LISE MEITNER
Discoverer of Nuclear Fission

Great Scientists

LISE MEITNER
Discoverer of Nuclear Fission

Rachel Stiffler Barron

MORGAN
REYNOLDS
Incorporated

Greensboro

LISE MEITNER
DISCOVERER OF NUCLEAR FISSION

Photo credits: AIP Emilio Segre Visual Archives

Library of Congress Cataloging-in-Publication Data:
Barron, Rachel
    Lise Meitner : discoverer of nuclear fission / Rachel Stiffler Barron.
        p. cm -- (Great Scientists)
    Includes bibliographical references and index.
    Summary: A biography of the Austrian scientist whose discoveries in nuclear physics
played a major part in developing atomic energy.
    ISBN 1-883846-52-8
        1. Meitner, Lise, 1878-1968--Juvenile literature. 2.
    Physicists--Germany--Biography--Juvenile literature. 3. Nuclear fission--Juvenile
    literature. [1. Meitner, Lise, 1878-1968. 2. Physicists. 3. Women--Biography] I. Title.
    II. Great scientists (Greensboro, N.C.)

QC774.M4 B37 2000
539.7'092--dc21
[B]

99-049724

Contents

Lise Meitner

Chapter One

Escape

On July 12, 1938, Lise Meitner started the day, routinely enough, by going to her job at the scientific institute where she had worked for almost thirty years. She tried to appear as though nothing was wrong, but she and a few of her closest friends knew a secret that could cost them their lives: this was to be Lise Meitner's last day in Germany.

At fifty-nine, she was one of the world's most renowned physicists. She had shunned the traditional route of marriage and children in favor of a career. She had chosen a field that few women even considered. And she had been very successful. She and her partner, the chemist Otto Hahn, had discovered a new chemical element, protactinium. Now she and Otto thought they might be on the verge of discovering another new element.

But she would have to leave all of that behind. Adolf Hitler and his Nazi Party had taken over Germany and other countries in Europe as well. Hitler and the Nazis hated Jews and wanted to annihilate them. They had forced many Jews out of their jobs. Some had emigrated to other countries, but those who had stayed were not even allowed to travel anymore.

Lise stayed at work until eight p.m., then left for home, where she hastily threw all she could into two small suitcases. She could not take any of her furniture or books or scientific papers. She could not withdraw any of her money from the bank, either. She could not tell anyone good-bye. All of those things would have tipped off the German officials that she was planning not just a short trip, but to flee the country permanently. They would arrest her and anyone else who was helping her.

Otto Hahn and his wife were among those helping Lise escape, and they feared for her safety and their own. Hitler's Storm Troopers often searched trains for Jews and arrested them. It would be easy for Lise to be caught if someone asked to see her passport. She did not have one, because the German government refused to give them to Jews. "We were shaking with fear whether she would get through or not," Otto would later say. That night, he gave Lise a diamond ring he had inherited from his mother, telling her to sell it if she became desperate for money.

The next day, Otto drove her to the train station. As she boarded the train, Lise was relieved to see a friend, Dirk Coster. They said hello to each other as though they had met by chance, but it was no coincidence. Dirk Coster and his wife, Miep, were helping Jews escape from Germany. The Costers were going to let Lise stay at their home in the Netherlands until she found another place to go.

It was a tense train ride. As they neared the border between Germany and the Netherlands, Lise's fear became almost unbearable. Trying to soothe her, Coster offered to hold on to the diamond ring for her. The train crossed over the border. No one came to ask Lise for her passport.

Hitler's officials read all the mail and telegrams that came into Germany, so Dirk Coster sent the Hahns a telegram in code saying that "the baby" had arrived safely. Hahn knew that meant that Lise's trip had been uneventful. He wrote back to Coster, in code, giving his "heartiest congratulations." He asked, "What will be the little daughter's name?"

It was only later that everyone understood how close Lise had come to being turned in to the German authorities. Kurt Hess, a Nazi scientist at the institute, had somehow learned she was planning to escape and had notified the government. Fortunately, two sympathetic police officers purposely delayed the investigation long enough for her to escape.

Otto went on with their experiments, with Lise offering advice in letters from her new home. Little did they know they were on the verge of discovering something that would alter the course of history: *nuclear fission*, or the splitting of the atom. Until that time, no one knew that an atom could split—and what awesome power it would unleash when it did.

Chapter Two

Gifted Young Woman

Elise Meitner was born in November 1878 in Vienna, Austria, to Philipp Meitner and his wife, Hedwig. For reasons we do not know, her name was eventually shortened only to Lise. There is uncertainty about her birth date as well. She would always celebrate November 7 as her birthday, but the birth registry of Vienna listed her as being born on November 17.

Vienna in those days was a carefree place, and such confusion over birth names and dates raised little concern. People settled there in droves, attracted by Vienna's beauty and its opera, theater, newspapers, good food, and vineyards. The Danube River flowed through the city, which was bounded by the Carpathian Mountains and the Alps.

But Vienna had a darker side, too. Many people were unable to find work. They did not have enough to eat, and there were water shortages and outbreaks of cholera in the summer. In fact, some of the city's residents were so poor that they shared beds, sleeping in shifts. The city was crowded and unsanitary, and it had the highest rate of suicide of any city in Europe.

The Meitner family, however, led a prosperous and comfortable life. Philipp was one of the Jews to benefit from social reforms instituted by Austria's ruler, Kaiser Franz Joseph. For the first time, Jews were allowed freedom of expression and worship. They were also given access to occupations from which they had been previously barred. Philipp became one of the city's first Jewish lawyers because of these new policies. The family lived close to a huge park where they could play and stroll on Sundays. Occasionally, they even saw the Kaiser himself riding by.

Although he never ran for office, Philipp was active in the Liberal political party, which came to power in Vienna and built an ample water supply and flood control. The party also improved public health, hospitals, and schools. Philipp and Hedwig opened their home to many interesting people—legislators, writers, chess players, and lawyers. Lise, the third of eight children, would always fondly remember staying up past her bedtime to listen to the boisterous conversations. Later, she would write that what she cherished most was the "unusual goodness of my parents, and the extraordinarily intellectual atmosphere in which my brothers and sisters and I grew up."

From the beginning, Lise had a passion for science and math. Her cousin, Otto Robert Frisch, described her as "an eight-year-old who kept a math book under

Petite, dark-eyed Hedwig Meitner supported her children's pursuit of higher education in nineteenth-century Vienna.

her pillow and would ask about the colors of an oil slick and remember what she was told about thin films and the interference effects of reflected light."

Unfortunately, education was limited for girls in Austria at that time. Their formal schooling ended at age fourteen, after which some middle-class girls were sent to private schools that prepared them for teaching, the only profession they could enter. Girls who were not lucky enough to go to these schools spent their teen years helping out at home and preparing for marriage.

Lise went to a private school and trained to be a French teacher, although she had little interest in teaching. In Austria, most people believed that if women were subjected to a rigorous university education like men, they would suffer mental illness, infertility, or some other social catastrophe. Fortunately, that attitude was eroding, and universities were finally beginning to admit women just as Lise and her sisters came of age.

There was still another roadblock, however. Because the Austrian school system had not given women adequate preparation for college work, Lise and her sisters had to have private tutoring to get them ready for the university. They crammed as much as eight years' worth of study in Greek, Latin, mathematics, physics, botany, zoology, mineralogy, psychology, logic, religion, German literature, and history into two years.

Then Lise had to endure a terrifying exam in order to prove she was qualified to enter a university. Of

Philipp Meitner benefitted from the social reforms implemented by Kaiser Franz Joseph and became one of Vienna's first Jewish lawyers.

fourteen young women who took the exam, which was given by strange teachers they had never met, only four, including Lise, passed.

As an adult, Lise wrote how grateful she was to her parents for their support: "Many parents shared the prejudice of the time against [women's] education, so that their daughters either had to forgo the education they desired, or fight for it." She told of one friend who, at age twenty-four, wanted to be privately tutored to prepare for the university. Her parents, "in other respects very loving—I'm sure—literally kept her prisoner in their apartment to keep her from carrying out her intentions. Only when she disappeared from the apartment one day and let her parents know that she would not return unless she had permission to study, did they give in."

At the age of twenty-three, Lise entered the University of Vienna. She was small and slender, with a faraway expression and serious dark eyes. She was an intense student who immediately plunged into college-level physics, calculus, chemistry, and botany. Desperate to make up for lost time, she enrolled in a heavy load of classes. Consequently, she was often very tired. She said, "I was really afraid I would slip off my chair" in the middle of the lectures.

One subject that always kept her awake was physics, which is the branch of science that searches for the ultimate laws of the universe by studying the forms of

In her early twenties, Lise Meitner passed a rigorous exam in order to apply for admission to the University of Vienna.

matter and energy and how they interact together. Physics requires an indepth understanding of very complex math. It was one of the most difficult courses of study she could have chosen. At the time, there were only about 700 physicists teaching in colleges and universities in both the United States and Austria combined, and very few worked in business or industry. The fact that Lise chose to study physics placed her in a very small group of students, an environment where she could receive a lot of individual attention.

All of her physics classes were taught by one professor, Ludwig Boltzmann, a big, heavy man with curly brown hair and a reddish beard. Unlike many professors, he had great confidence in what women could achieve and had encouraged the university to accept them. His enthusiasm for physics was immediately evident in the way he lectured. He poured himself into his teaching, pledging to give his students "all I have: myself, my entire way of thinking and feeling." In return, though, he demanded the same dedication from the students: "your trust, your affection, your love —in a word, for the most you have the power to give, yourself."

Boltzmann, who was fifty-eight years old, was a legend in physics. He had been a pioneer in describing the atom and how it works—theories that are an accepted part of science classes today. At the time, however, most scientists didn't even believe the atom existed.

Ludwig Boltzmann was Lise's physics professor at the University of Vienna. Boltzmann encouraged all of his female students to succeed.

No one had seen an atom, even with a microscope, and scientists who called themselves "positivists" refused to believe in anything they could not directly observe.

Much of Boltzmann's work involved kinetic theory, or explaining how the movements of a material's atoms and molecules contribute to its behavior. For example, kinetic theory states that it is the constant impact of atoms and molecules hitting against the inside of a gas tank that causes pressure to build up in the tank.

Boltzmann and those who believed his theories often found themselves in heated arguments with the positivists. They also had to compete against the positivists for teaching positions and respect. Fortunately for Boltzmann, discoveries just a few years later erased any doubt about the atom's existence.

Despite his achievements, Boltzmann was not above admitting his mistakes. He would shrug and laugh, saying, "Ach, how dumb of me," when he made a mistake on the blackboard. He created an environment for Lise and other women students that was free of the obstacles they had endured so far. Boltzmann, she later wrote, was a "'pure soul,' full of goodness of heart, idealism, and reverence for the wonder of the natural order of things."

By the summer of 1905, after three years at the university, Lise completed her coursework. In Austrian universities, a student could earn a doctorate by completing several months of research. Lise's research pro-

Marie Curie won the Nobel Prize for Physics, (1903) and Chemistry, (1911).

ject involved heat conduction and greatly impressed her professors. In February 1906, after passing a rigorous oral exam, she received her doctorate and graduated *summa cum laude*.

Just as the career of Dr. Lise Meitner was beginning, the life of her mentor ended. Boltzmann, who had been plagued by severe bouts of depression for years and had attempted suicide several times, finally succeeded in ending his life. His legacy lived on with his students, including Lise Meitner. She was more determined than ever to pursue a career in physics, the field Boltzmann loved. Boltzmann's own struggle to prove his theories demonstrated to Lise that science was about more than cold, objective experiments—that it depended upon human creativity and judgment as well.

For a few months after her graduation, Lise was not sure what she would do next. There were virtually no positions for women scientists. Even Marie Curie, who made ground-breaking discoveries about radioactivity and became the first woman to win the Nobel Prize in 1903, continued to endure the discrimination that all women scientists of that era suffered.

Lise could not have imagined where her new career would take her. Physics as we know it today includes the study of such phenomena as electricity, electronics, and magnetism. It also includes a field that did not yet exist: nuclear physics.

Chapter Three

Young Scientist

In Austria at the time there were no jobs for women in universities, so Lise Meitner took a position as a teacher in a girls' school. She did not really enjoy it, and each night she returned to the cluttered and run-down physics building at the University of Vienna to help a young scientist named Stefan Meyer with his experiments.

After Boltzmann's death, Meyer had become the director of the Physics Institute. He had already earned recognition for investigating the magnetic properties of some new elements that Marie Curie and her husband, Pierre, had just discovered: polonium, radium, and actinium.

The study of *radiation* was an exciting new field. Only ten years before, in 1896, a French scientist named Henri Becquerel discovered that the element uranium emitted an invisible radiation that penetrated paper and exposed photographic plates. A few years later, Ernest Rutherford—who is known for discovering the atomic nucleus—and his team of scientists classified radiation into three different types.

One type was hardly strong enough to pass through a sheet of paper. It was called *alpha* radiation. Another type could penetrate aluminum to a depth of three millimeters. It was named *beta* radiation. A third, very powerful type could pass through lead bricks several centimeters thick. It was named *gamma* radiation.

Today there is much concern about exposure to radiation. Exposure can be fatal to humans in both the long and short term. The early scientists who worked with radiation, including Lise, did not realize this. They wore no protective clothing and did not attempt to shield themselves in any way. Remarkably, despite her many years of work with radiation, Lise lived almost to the age of ninety.

Lise used a primitive piece of equipment called a *leaf electroscope* to measure radiation. It was nothing more than a metal rod with a very thin leaf of gold or aluminum fastened to it. When the rod was given an electric charge, the gold leaf was repelled away from the rod. When a radioactive substance was brought near, however, the leaf would fall back to its resting position. By measuring how quickly this happened, scientists could determine the strength of a particular element's radioactivity.

These experiments fascinated Lise and fueled her desire to be a full-time physicist. She remembered that Boltzmann had talked glowingly of the university in Berlin, Germany. Boltzmann said that while the best thinkers in physics were Austrian, the best equipment was in Germany.

Lise asked her parents to support her financially while she attended a few terms of classes at the Friedric-Wilhelm-Universitat in Berlin. Although her parents agreed, Lise felt terribly guilty for asking. At the age of twenty-eight, she was tired of having to depend on them for an allowance.

Lise arrived in Berlin, the intellectual, political, and social center of Germany, in 1907. Like Vienna, it had large public hospitals, clinics, museums, churches, palaces, libraries, and theaters. Although Berlin did not have the charming architecture, delicious food, and stylish women's clothing that Austrians enjoyed, it did have an energy and vitality that made it an exciting new home.

Unfortunately, women dealt with even more discrimination in Germany than in Austria. They were expected to be content with being virtuous housewives and mothers. There were even fewer women at the Berlin university than there had been in Vienna. Lise had always been shy, and the overwhelmingly male atmosphere made her even more withdrawn.

Lise had to ask permission to attend classes. The man who reluctantly gave it was Max Planck. When Lise arrived, Planck was not as open-minded about having women in the university as Boltzmann had been. He believed that, while a few women deserved exceptions, "it can not be emphasized strongly enough that Nature itself has designated for woman her vocation as mother and housewife, and that under no circumstances can natural laws be ignored without grave damage, which in this case would appear especially in the next generation."

There were some men in the university who felt differently. One of them was a young chemist named Otto Hahn. Otto was the same age as Lise, and he was the only person in the university's Chemistry Institute who worked with the new field of radioactivity. He was anxious to find a partner and was thrilled to hear of Lise's experience.

The two hit it off immediately. Otto's informal, easy-going manner helped Lise overcome her shyness. Otto had never studied mathematics and physics, so Lise's knowledge was invaluable to him. But again, there was a roadblock to their working together. The Chemistry Institute was closed to women.

Emil Fischer, the director, feared that women scientists might catch their hair on fire during experiments or suffer some other cataclysm. He grudgingly agreed to let Lise work in a room in the basement, but only because it had a separate entrance. There was no women's bathroom in the building, so she had to walk to a restaurant down the street. Fortunately, the ban on women in universities was lifted a year later. In response, Fischer finally welcomed them and installed

In 1907, Max Planck believed that it was unnatural for women to leave home and study in a university.

a women's bathroom.

Lise and Otto's first experiments together involved measuring and studying beta radiation, which scientists did not know much about. When Lise went home to Vienna for summer vacation, she asked her parents to give her the money to stay another year. Once again, her parents supported her wholeheartedly.

While she was in Vienna, Lise formally withdrew from the Jewish community and was baptized as a Protestant. Two of her sisters had already done the same. In fact, the entire Meitner family, although they were of Jewish ethnic origin, did not practice the religion.

Back in Berlin in the fall, Lise and Otto made their first significant discovery as a team.

At the time, scientists already knew that radiation is caused when the nucleus of an atom breaks down or *decays*. They knew that the nucleus of an atom contained *protons*, which have a positive charge, and that *electrons*, which have a negative charge, orbit around the nucleus.

When a nucleus emits alpha radiation, it loses two protons. The original nucleus is called the "parent", and the resulting nucleus after the decay is called the "daughter".

Lise and Otto discovered that when a radioactinium atom expels an alpha particle, it does so with such force that the daughter atom, known as actinium X, recoils,

After her arrival in Berlin, Lise began conducting beta radiation experiments with Otto Hahn.

much as a rifle recoils after firing a bullet. Sometimes the force of this recoil could send the daughter atom spiraling away from the parent.

Lise and Otto showed that scientists could purposely cause this recoil to occur in the laboratory, which would allow them to produce purer and larger samples of radioactive substances for their experiments. It also made it easier for scientists to test the half-life of a particular substance, or the length of time it takes for half of its nucleus to decay.

Even though Otto and Lise had worked together only a short time, their collaboration already had produced successful results. When Ernest Rutherford and his wife visited Berlin, Rutherford had already read the articles they had published about their work. When he met Lise he was startled. "Oh, I thought you were a man," he exclaimed.

Everyone, including Lise, laughed at Rutherford's mistake. Lise then had to take Rutherford's wife shopping instead of joining in on the discussion while the two men talked about physics. In a letter to a friend, Rutherford jokingly mentioned that Lise was "a young lady but not beautiful so I judge Hahn will not fall a victim to the radioactive charms of the lady."

Lise was not beautiful, but she was not unattractive. Although she was shy, she had a warm personality and made friends easily. But she and Otto remained only friends. They were careful to avoid even the appear-

After reading the articles Lise and Otto published about beta radiation, Ernest Rutherford mistook "L. Meitner" for a man.

ance of anything more, since they were aware that everyone at the Chemistry Institute was watching them closely. It was unusual for a man and a woman to be professional partners, spending all day alone together in a room.

Otto would later write that Lise "had had a strict ladylike upbringing and was very reserved, even shy... we generally worked until nearly eight in the evening, so that one or the other of us would have to go out to buy salami or cheese before the shops shut at that hour. We never ate our cold supper together there. Lise Meitner went home alone, and so did I. And yet we were really very close friends."

Lise and Otto continued their work, although as a woman Lise was not paid. Her parents continued sending her an allowance, and she wrote articles under the name of "L. Meitner" for extra money. She used only her first initial because she knew that many publications would not accept articles written by women. In fact, one editor of an encyclopedia told her he "would not think of printing an article by a woman!"

Lise lived frugally, renting rooms in which she shared a bathroom with others. She listed her clothing as "7 blouses, 20 pair stockings, 4 underskirts..." and pinched every penny. She ate very little so that she would have money for a daily newspaper and concerts.

Otto supported Lise's work wholeheartedly and persuaded her to overcome her shyness enough to give talks to other scientists about her work. At one conference at which she spoke in Vienna, she met young Albert Einstein. Einstein and Lise were both thirty, but he had already published his revolutionary *theory of relativity*. Lise sat transfixed as he lectured about it.

Even as a man, Otto did not earn much money because radioactivity, his specialty, was so new and unappreciated. Finally, in 1905, the rest of the scientific community recognized how important radioactivity was. A new, more modern and spacious Kaiser-Wilhelm-Institut (KWI) for Physical Chemistry and Electrochemistry was built in Dahlem, a suburb of Berlin, and a section of the building was devoted to radioactivity, the first of its kind in Germany. At last, Otto was offered a good position with a respectable salary. Lise, however, was invited to join him as an "unpaid guest."

The continued struggles Lise experienced as a woman in physics would have discouraged others, and at times Lise herself wondered if she would ever truly succeed. Then, suddenly, Max Planck, who had only grudgingly accepted the idea of women even attending the university five years before, appointed her his assistant. This position was the first rung on the academic ladder, and opened up the possibility that Lise could advance to eventually become a full professor. Finally, she would be paid for her work. It could not have come at a better time. Her father, who had so generously supported her dreams, had passed away.

She wrote jubilantly to her friend from the university, Elizabeth Schiemann: "I love physics with all my heart. I can hardly imagine it not being part of my life. It is a kind of personal love, as one has for a person to whom one is grateful for many things."

Lise's enthusiasm and determination had sustained her in a foreign country, through poverty, and in a world dominated by men. It had inspired her to overcome her shyness. She would always be grateful to physics for giving her those things. At long last, she was sure she had chosen the right path.

Chapter Four

The War to End All Wars

Exciting things were happening for both Lise and Otto. In 1912, Otto married Edith Junghans, a pretty art student. In 1913, Lise was thrilled to learn that she was to receive a promotion. The radioactivity section of the KWI was renamed after both of them: the Laboratorium Hahn-Meitner. Although she now held the same position as Otto, Lise was still paid less because she was a woman.

When the institute moved to a new building, Lise and Otto decided to take steps to limit radioactive contamination—although it was not for health reasons. In their old building, radioactivity from spills had reached the point that it interfered with their radiation measurements.

In the new building, Lise and Otto said that chemical experiments would be done in rooms other than those where measurements were taken. Everyone handling a radioactive substance had to touch telephones and door handles with a piece of toilet paper! Rolls of toilet paper hung in various places around the building for this purpose.

It was not long, however, before world events overtook their experiments.

For decades, Germany and Austria-Hungary had had a smoldering conflict with the Bosnians who lived in the country of Serbia. In June 1914, a gang of Serbs assassinated Austria's Archduke Franz Ferdinand, nephew of the beloved Kaiser and heir to the throne.

The small band of Serbs had not acted on behalf of the Serbian goverment and did not represent the views of the Serbian people, and a punishment for the murderers could have been worked out without dragging nations into war. But Austria-Hungary wanted an excuse to attack the Serbs. There were no serious attempts to reach a peaceful agreement.

Within a week Germany had joined Austria-Hungary against the Serbs, and soon the whole continent of Europe was at war. There were numerous causes for World War I. One was the fear that many Europeans had toward Germany. The Germans did not understand how much other Europeans feared them. Instead, Germany itself felt threatened. Most Germans believed, with the exception of Austria-Hungary, that they were surrounded by "enemies." Most Germans were enthusiastic about an opportunity to assure their country's dominance in Europe. They saw this war as necessary to protect their country's future. Austrian, Hungarian, and German men jubilantly marched off to war in parades, expecting to be home after a quick and decisive victory by Christmas. Those who stayed behind, including Lise, rallied patriotically behind the cause.

During a visit to Vienna, Lise wrote to her friend, Elisabeth: "My mother's apartment is directly across from the train station and each day I see the men going off to war with unbelievable enthusiasm. Those who remain behind outdo themselves in demonstrating love for those who are leaving, and the train station presents a festive, joyous sight all day long."

One of those men was Otto. It wasn't long before he and his fellow soldiers saw a less than glamorous side of war. During the invasion of Belgium, Otto saw civilians killed in the town of Louvain. The Germans set fire to Gothic monuments and even burned down a library dating to medieval times. Still, Otto enjoyed the camaraderie of serving in the German Army. He, like most Germans, saw the war as necessary to protect Germany's future.

Lise, too, wanted to contribute to the war effort. She signed up for x-ray technician training and an anatomy course so that she could be in the medical corps. While taking these classes, she struggled to keep the most important experiments going without Otto, but it was difficult to stay focused with so much happening.

By the end of 1914, it was clear that the war would not end quickly, and that victory for Germany and

Austria-Hungary was anything but certain. But most German people, including the scientists, supported the war. One well-known scientist who did not was Albert Einstein. In fact, Einstein said that Germany was wrong and that he hoped it would be defeated.

Meanwhile, Otto was asked to join the Pioneer Regiment, a special military unit that was creating chemical weapons. Otto and others questioned whether this was a humane thing to be involved in. Fritz Haber—who had developed the chemical weapons—assured them that France had already used poison gas, and so Germany would have to use it to defend itself.

Otto wrote to Lise about his reservations. Although she understood little about chemical weapons, she wanted to support her friend. "First, you were not asked (but ordered), and second, if you do not do it, someone else will," she wrote to him. "Above all, any means which might help shorten this horrible war are justified."

A few months later, Otto saw firsthand the horror that gases could inflict. He watched as Russian soldiers died painful and agonizing deaths. Still, he continued his work with the Pioneer Regiment.

The fighting dragged on. In the summer of 1915, Lise left for Lemberg, near the Austrian-Russian border, to join a medical corps on the battle front there.

Her experience in the medical corps would change

her view of war forever. The suffering of the soldiers was almost unbearable. She wrote to Elisabeth: "I never expected it to be as awful as it actually is. These poor people, who at best will be cripples, have the most horrible pains. One can hear their screams and groans as well as see their horrible wounds. Since we are only about 40 km from the front we get only the most severely wounded here. I tell myself this for consolation. But one has one's own thoughts about war when one sees all this."

The medical unit had hastily converted a technical school into a hospital, and the x-ray equipment was not even ready. In the meantime, Lise helped out any way she could, assisting in operations, cleaning the operating tables and instruments, and bandaging the wounded. Her letters to Elisabeth showed her growing despair: "Today we amputated the foot of a very young Hungarian, and it upset me that I could say nothing to him [because she did not speak the language]...A young Polish soldier said quietly, 'I know I will die,' and he did."

Lise wrote nothing of her romantic life in her memoirs or her letters, but among her belongings, her family later found a letter from a Greek professor that was mailed to her at the hospital. In purple ink and flowery handwriting, he wrote: "I would like to have the honor of marrying you. I admire you and the other Germans and your wonderful country. I hope you take my offer of marriage seriously. Also I would like your photograph. Please answer me. P.S. Greece is now all for the Germans."

It is uncertain whether Lise ever answered him, but we know that she did not accept his offer. She may have received other offers of marriage during her life, but she never mentioned them. When she was older, a friend would ask her why she never married, to which she only replied, laughing: "I never had time for it!"

Lise's first love in life was physics, something she missed terribly during the war. She felt useless and discouraged that she could not save the suffering and dying soldiers. In August 1916, she wrote to Elisabeth: "I feel superfluous. Without me things would go just as well. If this is true, then my duty is to go back to the Kaiser Wilhelm Institute. I say my duty because if I had followed my wishes, I would have gone back long ago."

In September, Lise was back in Berlin, ready to pick up the pieces of the research she and Otto had begun. Their latest project related to uranium once again. Often, scientists had noticed that in minerals containing the element uranium, the element actinium was also present. They never found actinium without uranium, which led them to suspect that uranium would somehow decay into actinium. No one was able to make this happen in a laboratory, however. Like many others, Lise and Otto suspected that there was an intermediate element—a "mother substance" in the decay chain, and they set out to try to find it.

During several short leaves from the army, Otto joined in on the experiments. For the most part, though, Lise continued alone. Most of the students, assistants, and technicians were off fighting.

In April 1917, the United States joined England, France, and Russia (or the Allies) in the war against Germany and Austria-Hungary. The scientists who were left spent much of their time working on projects to help the military, something Lise feared she might be required to do also.

Fortunately, that did not happen. Instead, she was given another promotion and more responsibility. In fact, the Laboratorium Hahn-Meitner was now split into the Laboratorium Hahn and the Laboratorium Meitner. Lise was now head of her own section. Her experiments were becoming more difficult, however, because so many materials had been sent to help the military. Lise and Otto hunted for uranium and actinium in a mineral called pitchblende, but they needed significant amounts of it for their experiments. Lise spent a great deal of time and effort swapping materials, and even pleading with other scientists to get it.

The war had begun to affect the entire population. Food and fuel were scarce. In Otto's letters to Lise, he expressed concern that she might not be eating enough. In her characteristic selflessness, she brushed his worries aside. Otherwise, their letters were long and enthusiastic, discussing the progress of the experiments. Finally, Otto received a jubilant letter from Lise dated January 17, 1918. She had finally succeeded in isolating the mother substance.

It was their second major discovery, and Lise and Otto submitted a paper about it to a scientific journal. "We have succeeded in discovering a new radioactive element, and demonstrating that it is the mother substance of actinium," they wrote. "We propose, therefore, the name protactinium."

In the summer of 1918, German citizens finally learned the sobering truth: the war had cost 1.7 million German lives and another 1.2 million lives in Austria-Hungary. New, powerful machine guns and tanks that made this war the most devastating the world had ever seen.

The German troops were out of fuel. The men and their horses were near starvation. The two countries had little choice but to sign an armistice with the Allies on November 11, 1918. With the signing of the armistice, the bloodiest war that the world had ever known—the one that had been called the "war to end all wars"—came to a close.

In Germany and Austria-Hungary there was chaos. The Kaiser fled Germany, fearing he would be overthrown by a military coup. Rival factions fought with each other in the streets for control of the government.

Neither Austria-Hungary nor Germany would ever again be ruled by nobility. They had suffered a humiliating defeat in the war. But Lise, always an optimist, told her friends that everything would be fine.

Otto returned, and he and Lise continued their work. Protactinium, with the symbol Pa, became element ninety-one on the periodic table of elements. Although Lise had done nearly all of the work, she allowed Otto's name to appear as the "senior author" of their papers. Perhaps she felt this was a way of honoring a soldier who had served his country. In any case, she was a loyal friend.

Later, Otto would not prove to be as loyal to Lise.

Chapter Five

Difficult Peace

Although the war was over, Germany and Austria were in a state of despair. Germany had not only lost the war, but it was also punished severely by the peace settlement. The winter of 1919 was another hungry and cold one. In Vienna, people were literally starving to death. Lise's old friend Stefan Meyer wrote to her: "Milk and meat are unknown words, coal is nonexistent, wood insufficient and expensive."

At least Lise could be happy that her career was going well, for she finally attained the rank of professor—the first woman to do so in Germany. Being a professor, however, did not automatically mean that a person could teach students. The new professor also had to demonstrate impressive research, and given her ground-breaking work with Otto, this was a requirement that Lise easily met.

Her fame was also growing abroad. She was invited to Sweden to lecture about radioactivity at the University of Lund, where little was known about the subject. She was a hit with the students, who gave her

In 1919, Lise attained the title of professor.

a bouquet of flowers and saluted her by giving humorous speeches on her last day. Lise used her time in Sweden to learn more about the developing field of *x-ray spectroscopy*, or the study of x-ray wavelengths. She also made a new friendship with Dirk Coster, a young scientist, and his wife, Miep.

Lise's achievements were not always properly recognized. The Association of German Chemists awarded Otto the Emil Fischer Medal, its highest honor, but it only gave Lise a copy of Otto's medal—not one of her own. If she was disappointed, Lise hid it well. She congratulated Otto and told him she thought he was very deserving of the award. She was apparently resigned to the fact that it was nearly impossible for a woman to be regarded as anything more than a male scientist's assistant.

In Germany, inflation was so bad that the mark was practically worthless. It took wheelbarrows-full of them to pay a scientist's salary for one pay period. On pay day, Lise and her colleagues would stuff the marks into suitcases, then rush out to buy food and supplies—before their value could drop even further. Most people did not have enough money to buy heating fuel for their homes and offices, either. Lise shivered from the cold at home and at the institute, which was having a difficult time buying equipment and supplies for experiments. Lise was tired of living in a small rented room, but she could not afford a larger apartment. Scientists had no money to travel to conferences or, in some cases, to even take a taxi across the city of Berlin.

In November 1923, the German people grew so desperate that riots broke out in the street, and the National Socialist Party, or the Nazis, attempted to overthrow the government. They were unsuccessful, and their leader, Adolf Hitler, was sentenced to five years in prison. He actually served only nine months, but while there he began writing a book detailing his political philosophies.

The book, *Mein Kampf* (German for *My Struggle*), revealed the mind of a very disturbed man. Hitler wrote that he was going to help Germany reclaim its lost glory, that he would lead the Germans to claim their rightful place as the leaders of the world. Germans, he wrote, were a superior race of people, and they must remain "pure" by not intermarrying with Jews or Slavic peoples. He was particularly critical of the Jews, who he said were ethically and morally corrupt.

At the time, the trials of everyday life seemed much more distressing than Hitler's book. Through her letters, Lise tried to reassure her mother that she was doing well. "There really is enough to eat, although the prices are completely crazy; a kilogram of margarine costs 30 to 40 million [marks], one egg costs 1 1/2 to 2 million, etc.," Lise wrote to her. "Personally, I feel fine... I myself don't mind if there is less to eat. It's much worse for ill people and children—no milk, hardly any butter. In the laboratories the workshops are open only from 9-11 and 5-7 because it's so cold." Every two weeks, Lise's mother sent her a package with coffee and sometimes a nutcake. Then, in December 1924, she passed away.

Lise's nephew, Otto Robert Frisch, had received a doctorate in physics and moved to Berlin to take a research position there. The two visited often, playing piano duets together for fun and attending symphony concerts.

The field of physics was in a "golden age." It seemed there were new discoveries almost daily. Lise kept up with all of them, reading about the work of others and writing about it in scientific journals. By now she had more than forty articles to her name.

In 1930, Lise and a fellow physicist, Hans Geiger, received a letter from a friend, the scientist Wolfgang Pauli. Pauli's sense of humor showed in the letter, for he addressed it "Dear Radioactives."

Pauli wrote that he believed there might be an as-yet-unnamed particle in the nucleus of the atom that had neither a positive nor a negative charge. He proposed calling this particle a *neutron*. "At the moment I don't trust myself enough to publish anything about this idea and turn confidently to you, dear radioactives, with the question of how one might experimentally prove such a neutron...because if neutrons do exist they should certainly have been observed long ago!"

Lise welcomed her nephew Otto Robert Frisch's move to Berlin. Frisch was a physicist also.

Lise and other physicists around the world rose to the challenge. For her own experiments, Lise built a Wilson cloud chamber, the first one in Berlin. The cloud chamber had been invented by C. T. R. Wilson around 1900 for the study of clouds and mist.

Lise's chamber was only twenty-one centimeters in diameter. It was a sealed chamber filled with moist, dense, cloud-like air. Tiny water droplets would form on any nuclei, dust, or atoms inside the chamber. As these particles rapidly moved through the chamber, they formed visible tracks in the mist. By rigging up a camera that would take pictures inside the chamber, Lise was able to observe the behavior of atoms and their nuclei. She hoped that this would be a way for her to see a neutron, if indeed it existed.

Another new theory being batted about was that the atom contained vast amounts of untapped energy. Ernest Rutherford talked and wrote often about the enormous potential of energy inside the atom. He pointed out that the energy released during radioactive decay was much greater than a chemical reaction—that radium, for example, released energy a million times greater during radioactive decay than when it was actually burned as coal. The scientist F. W. Aston mused that some day "the human race will have at its command powers beyond the dreams of science fiction."

Another scientist, James Chadwick, was the first to discover the neutron. But the excitement had helped

Wolfgang Pauli proposed that a non-charged particle, or *neutron*, existed inside the nucleus of the atom.

distract Lise from the troubling times in Germany. There were endless power struggles as various parties were elected to power, failed to solve Germany's enormous problems, then were voted out of office.

The unrest allowed Hitler and his Nazi Party, with their promises to restore Germany to glory, to come to power. The Nazis did not hesitate to use violence against Jews or anyone else who opposed them.

On January 30, 1933, Lise and her friend Annemarie Schrodinger listened to the radio in horror as Hitler was sworn in as chancellor of Germany. By now Hitler even had his own private army that was larger than the official German army. It was called the "SS," or the Brownshirts. Hitler called the new government the "Third Reich," meaning the Third Empire. The first empire had been the Holy Roman Empire; the second, the German empire that had been decimated by the war. Now Germany was to become powerful once again.

A little more than a month later, the first elections were held. They were anything but democratic. The Brownshirts swarmed all over Berlin, beating, arresting, even murdering people who were campaigning for the opposing party. Even with all this, the Nazis failed to win a majority in parliament.

Lise tried not to be alarmed. Otto was spending several months as a guest lecturer at Cornell University in Ithaca, New York, and Lise wrote to him: "The political situation is rather strange, but I very much hope it will take a calmer, more sensible turn." She added that the institute was going to be required to fly the Nazi swastika flag. She was careful not to be too critical because the Nazis had already begun reading mail that went in and out of the country.

One of the Nazis' first official acts was to declare a one-day boycott against all Jewish businesses, even doctors and dentists. Of course, many ordinary Germans did not support the boycott, but it was obvious that anyone who chose to go against it did so at their own risk. Even the official German police could not protect the Jews and their supporters anymore.

Hitler wanted to purge Jews from every aspect of German life: from government, from the legal profession, from medicine, and even from education and the arts. The truth was that Jews made up less than one percent of the German population, but they comprised twenty percent of its scientists and twenty-five percent of its physicists.

The Nazis wanted to make an example out of Albert Einstein, who was a Jew. They planned to fire him from his job at the Prussian Academy of Sciences in Germany. On a visit to California, however, Einstein read about the upheaval in Germany in the newspapers. He announced to the press that he would not return to Germany. Instead, he sailed to Belgium, where he set up a new home and declared that he was resigning from his position with the academy.

Even more disturbing was the fact that, in Germany, few scholars and scientists came forward to defend Einstein. This angered Einstein even more, and he vowed to never set foot in Germany again. "The conduct of German intellectuals—as a group—was no better than the rabble," he would later say.

Jewish teachers and professors were dismissed from their jobs in droves, yet their non-Jewish colleagues, and even their students, did not protest. In fact, student activists were wearing brown shirts to class and demonstrating in support of the Nazis. They jeered and interrupted Jewish professors' lectures and organized bonfires at which they burned books by Jewish authors. In just one such book burning in Berlin, 20,000 books went up in flames. At the Kaiser Wilhelm Institute for Chemistry, Lise had to work alongside Professor Kurt Hess, who headed the organic chemistry section. Hess had a reputation for being a fanatical Nazi; he was also Lise's next-door neighbor.

Most ordinary Germans welcomed the new nationalist spirit that was sweeping Germany. The years of depression, hunger, and unemployment had taken their toll, and Germans were happy to see the country on the move again. Even those who were bothered by the things that were happening accepted it quietly.

Although Lise had declared herself a Protestant years before and had cared for Germany's wounded soldiers during the war, she was forced to fill out a paper in which she had to state that her grandparents had been Jewish. She began to wonder if she, like Einstein, should resign and leave Germany.

But the decision was a very emotional one. She considered Germany her home. Her cherished work in physics and nearly all of her friends were in Germany. She clung to the hope that she would not be dismissed from her job. As an Austrian citizen living in Germany, she might remain immune to these absurd new German policies.

Surely, she thought, this madness would soon end, and everyone would come to their senses.

Chapter Six

Years of Fear and Frustration

Fear of what was happening in Germany kept Lise awake at night. It was difficult to concentrate on physics.

Four thousand miles away, at Cornell University, Otto Hahn read about what was happening in Germany in the American and Canadian newspapers. He refused to believe most of it. He gave an interview to the *Toronto Star Weekly* in which he defended Hitler and Germany. The policies toward Jews, he said, were justified as part of Germany's policy of oppressing communists. The headline on the article read: "He Defends Hitler; Denies Man Who 'Lives Like a Saint' Is Guilty of the Atrocities Charged."

Letters from Lise and his wife, Edith, convinced Otto that the rumors were true. He cut short his stay in the United States to return to Germany. He found the institute in utter disarray. Fritz Haber, the head of the KWI, had resigned rather than carry out the goverment orders to fire all the Jewish scientists.

Now Otto was named the director, and he faced the same dilemma. Although he opposed the Nazis and refused to join their party, he had to agree to certain conditions in order to keep Lise and a few other Jewish scientists on the staff. These included flying the Nazi swastika flag in front of the building and praising Hitler in all of the institute's letters by including the words "Heil Hitler!"

The quality of scientific work in Germany was now beginning to suffer because many of the country's best scientists had been ousted from their jobs. Several of the most prominent Jewish scientists followed Einstein's lead and left the country to take posts in the United States and England.

Lise and others who remained knew they would eventually have to make a difficult decision. Should they abandon their work, and a country they loved, and let it be overrun by this evil? Or should they hang on, waiting for the day when the madness would end? Lise chose the latter path, thinking that as long as she could keep working, she would stay in Germany. Besides, the scientific community disdained participation in politics, believing that science should be kept pure of such interference. Perhaps if they remained quiet and unthreatening to the Reich, they would be left alone. It disturbed them, however, that the Nazis were now benefitting from their work.

In September 1933, orders from the government

took away Lise's right to teach at the University of Berlin. It did not affect her research, however, and that was what meant the most to her. Although he was quiet about his anti-Nazi views, even Otto could tell he was being slighted in favor of other scientists who were Nazi Party members. Still, the Third Reich realized that scientific research could only bring prestige to Germany.

Elsewhere, the golden age of physics continued. In 1934, American physicist Enrico Fermi reported yet another new discovery. He and his team had been bombarding the element uranium with neutrons. Although uranium was considered to be the heaviest element in the world, Fermi's experiments produced several new beta-emitting substances that he thought might be new, even heavier, elements. These became tentatively known as *transuranics*.

Lise, reading about Fermi's work, was enthralled. The rush was on, worldwide, as teams of scientists tried experiments designed to determine if they were indeed new elements.

Otto was not so enthusiastic, but Lise needed a chemist to help, and she persuaded him to join in. They also invited another chemist, Fritz Strassman, to join their team.

The experiments were long and tedious. They involved poking around in a radioactive mixture and searching for tiny amounts of radioactivity. Their

American physicist Enrico Fermi's "transuranics" were an important clue to the puzzle of nuclear fission.

results seemed to support Fermi's conclusion. The new substances did not appear to be any of the elements known at that time. By the end of 1934, Lise, Otto, and Fritz published an article saying that the new substances must indeed be transuranics. Further experiments made them even more confident. They published two more articles in 1936 and 1937, saying that there was "no doubt" that transuranics existed and that there was "no need for further discussion" on the matter. Otto's name was listed as the senior author of these articles, too, although Lise and Fritz had been just as responsible for the team's success.

But something about the transuranics bothered Lise. The decay chains seemed long and odd. As the decay chains progressed, the *atomic number*—the number of protons in the nucleus—kept rising. But the *mass number*, or the total number of protons *and* neutrons in the nucleus, stayed the same, which ran contrary to the laws of physics. Otto and Fritz were not bothered by this, but it troubled Lise.

Meanwhile, life in Germany was growing ever grimmer. On March 12, 1938, Hitler's German troops poured over the border into Austria. The Austrians welcomed Hitler with open arms. The police were voluntarily wearing brown shirts. Flags with swastikas were everywhere, even draped on the churches. Jubilantly, Hitler proclaimed that Austria would no longer be a separate country; it would now be a province of Germany. This event was called *Anschluss*, German for "annexation".

Then, suddenly, the celebration turned bloody. Ordinary people of Austria, inflamed with passion at Hitler's speeches, turned on their Jewish neighbors, dragging them out of their homes and beating and robbing them. Many Jews were killed, and some committed suicide. The rest of the world was horrified at these atrocities. Even some Germans were surprised.

The day after the Anschluss, Kurt Hess made his dislike of Lise very plain. "The Jewess endangers the institute," he said.

Word of this reached Otto, who was beginning to fear for his own safety and that of the entire institute. He mentioned to Lise that she might consider resigning. Lise was hurt and angry that Otto would even make such a suggestion.

Lise knew her job might end. Yet she really did not want to leave Germany. Emigration would require a great deal of preparation. She would have to get all of her personal affairs in order. She needed to write letters to friends in other countries to find out where she might get a job. And she needed to apply for a visa, something the German govenment might refuse to grant her.

For weeks, she was paralyzed with indecision. In the meantime, she kept working at the institute, although she no longer felt welcome. She began writing letters to her friends abroad about jobs, but she was careful not to be too blatant, because the Germans were reading the mail.

Her friends abroad knew about this, too. They wrote her letters inviting her to come to "conferences" or to be a "guest lecturer" at universities in Switzerland and Denmark. They were actually hinting that Lise should come under the guise of a temporary visit, then stay permanently. In April, Lise learned that the German Ministry of Education was now investigating her case. It was an ominous sign that her days at the institute were numbered.

On May 9, 1938, Lise reached her final decision. She wrote in her diary that she would go to Copenhagen, Denmark, to stay with her friends, Niels and Margrethe Bohr, until she could find a permanent home. Bohr had been awarded the 1913 Nobel Prize in Physics for his work in atomic theory. Otto Robert Frisch, her favorite nephew, was now working there with him.

Her hopes were dashed the next day. Denmark's embassy in Berlin denied her permission to go there. Now that Austria had been annexed into Germany, Lise's Austrian passport was no longer valid, so she would not be able to get back into Germany. Denmark did not want immigrants, and since Germany would not let her back in, they did not want her to come there, even temporarily.

Lise realized she was about to be hopelessly

trapped. The Germans would not let her work, but they were making it very difficult for her to leave, too. She applied for the travel papers from the German goverment anyway.

Meanwhile, a network of Lise's friends abroad began trying to find her a new job that would be suitable for a scientist of her accomplishments and that would pay a decent salary. Unfortunately, the best jobs had been filled by Jewish scientists who had already fled from Germany.

On June 16, Lise received the most foreboding news yet. A letter from the Ministry of the Interior said: "Political considerations are in effect that prevent the issuance of a passport for Frau Meitner to travel abroad. It is considered undesirable that well-known Jews leave Germany to travel abroad where they appear to be representatives of German science..."

Lise was devastated. Now it would be impossible for her to get out, even under the guise of going to a conference. If she could get out illegally, it appeared that Holland and Sweden were her only options for a new home. They were considered more lenient than other countries. But their governments still had to be persuaded that Lise's presence as a scientist would be an important benefit to them; neither would let her go there just for her own safety. And even if they let her in, she would not be permitted to work for pay.

Dirk Coster, whom Lise had befriended in 1921, and his friend, Dutch physicist Adriaan Fokker, began the process of convincing Holland's Minister of Justice and Minister of Education that Holland should accept Lise. In order to do this, they would have to show that there was an unpaid position available for her at a university. Then they would have to gather enough money from private donors for her to live on.

Coster and Fokker asked some wealthy Jewish industrialists in Holland to contribute money. They were not very successful. All of the donors had already been approached too many times by other Jews. One wrote that because so many of his personal friends and family members were also trying to flee Germany and Austria, "the demands on me are such that I am no longer free to offer philanthropic help to people outside my own circle."

Finally, a Swedish scientist offered Lise a one-year job at a new institute for nuclear research in Stockholm that was still under construction. Lise accepted. The Swedish had fallen behind in the new field of nuclear physics, and she believed she could be especially helpful to them.

The institute was not scheduled to open for several months, however, and Lise still needed to get out of Germany immediately. Coster and Fokker frantically phoned the Hague, the seat of the government in Holland, trying to find out if a decision had been made. On Monday morning, July 11, they heard the good news: Lise could come to Holland. Coster rushed to the

Dirk Coster helped Lise escape from Germany in 1938.

train station to leave for Berlin.

One of Coster's neighbors in Holland, E. H. Ebels, was an influential politician from a large farming family near the border of Germany and Holland. While Coster was on the train, Ebels got in his car and drove to the border station, where he showed the guards the permission papers for Lise to enter Holland.

Coster and Ebels had carefully chosen this particular station for a reason. The guards on the Holland side of the border were on good terms with the guards on Germany's side. Ebel and Coster believed that, of all the train stations along the border, this one was the most likely to let Lise pass through undisturbed. It was also not heavily traveled, which might make the guards there less suspicious.

Coster arrived in Berlin and spent Monday night with a friend, Peter Debye, and his family. He could not talk to Lise directly without arousing suspicion, so he explained the plan to Peter, who then relayed the message to Otto: Lise should be ready to leave first thing Wednesday morning.

When Lise arrived at work Tuesday morning, Otto pulled her aside and told her the news. Lise was filled with excitement and fear, but she had to pretend that nothing was out of the ordinary.

That night, she packed all she could into two small suitcases. Then she went to Otto's house to spend the night. It was difficult to tell who was more nervous—

Lise or Otto. "We were shaking with fear whether she would get through or not," Otto later said.

After thirty-one years in Germany, at the age of fifty-nine, Lise was being forced to leave her home, her career, and her friends. She could carry with her only a few clothes and a little bit of money. Otto, worried that she would run out of money, gave her a gift: a diamond ring he had inherited from his mother. Should she become desperate, he said, she could sell it for money to live on.

They agreed that if Lise crossed the border safely, she would send a coded telegram to Otto to let him know. "The danger consisted of the SS's repeated passport control of trains crossing the frontier," Otto later wrote. "People trying to leave Germany were always being arrested on the train and brought back." On Wednesday morning, Otto drove Lise to the train station and said good-bye. Lise boarded the train, Coster nodded to her and said hello. Lise pretended to be surprised, and sat down beside him.

As the train rumbled toward the border, Lise's nervousness was at times unbearable. When the train crossed quietly over the border, no one asked to see Lise's passport. For the first time in years, she was now out of danger.

But she felt as though her life had been wrenched from her. After many years of taking care of herself, she was now dependent upon others. She was terribly upset to learn that Coster and Fokker and their friends had pooled their own money to support her. She insisted that she would pay it back some day.

As hard as she tried not to show her frustration, her friends noticed. "Her sense of being inwardly torn apart is much worse than we can imagine," Fokker said. "She completely suppresses it; she speaks only about factual matters on the surface, but under the most severe tension."

And Lise's trials were not yet over. She felt nervous about the job in Sweden. She did not know anyone there or even speak the language. Her future was anything but certain.

Chapter Seven

Exile in Sweden

The strain of the situation in Germany had taken its toll not only on Lise, but on Otto and his family. Edith, his wife, was suffering from a nervous breakdown. His sixteen-year-old son, Hanno, was forced to join the Hitler Youth.

Meanwhile, Lise was experiencing more disappointments. Her position at the new Nobel Institute for Experimental Physics in Sweden was nothing close to what she had hoped it would be.

The new building was spacious and modern, but practically empty of scientific equipment. Manne Siegbahn, the director of the institute, said nothing more than hello to her on her first day at work. She learned, much to her dismay, that instead of a regular salary she was to be paid only a modest stipend from the Royal Swedish Academy of Sciences. With her bank account frozen in Berlin and nothing but thin summer clothes to wear as the weather grew colder, she was desperate to have her things sent from Berlin.

She wrote numerous letters to Otto, begging him to send her books, papers, and clothing.

Try as he might, Otto could not do this. The Education Ministry had become suspicious of Lise's departure, not believing Otto's story that she was only away temporarily. The ministry required that an inventory be taken of everything Lise owned and ordered that all of it, even her clothes, remain in Germany. The inventory revealed her modest belongings: "3 glass plates, 1 cigar cutter, 1 KWI [Kaiser Wilhelm Society for the Advancement of the Sciences] medal, 1 Leibniz medal, 1 Emil Fischer Medal, 1 Stefan Meyer Medal, 2 linen towels, 2 toothbrush holders..."

Lise's lawyer in Berlin mailed her papers to fill out and sign that supposedly would allow her to retrieve her pension from the German government. Lise complained in a letter to Otto: "I am not at all impatient, but it seems everything is going wrong...everything at a snail's pace: just to get rid of me! I know, Hahnchen, that you have a lot to think about and that it is hard for you, but...after 30 years of work shall I be left without even a few books?...I beg you again, please don't be angry. If you only knew how my life now appears."

Meanwhile, the rest of the world watched Hitler with dread and fear. He was threatening to invade Czechoslovakia, and now England and France were considering declaring war against Germany. In a last-ditch effort to maintain peace, they decided to negotiate with Hitler. They allowed the German-speaking part of Czechoslovakia to go to Germany in return for Hitler's agreement not to push further.

Relieved, Lise wrote to Otto: "Hopefully now the world will be somewhat calmer...Please send my dresses and underwear soon. I need some of them urgently ...Good night dear Otto, and many thanks for everything."

Otto wrote back: "The laboratory is half deserted because many have gone to the reception for Hitler, as one is supposed to do. This past week there was in fact practically no work done, the anxiety was dreadful, and now we are, thank God, freed of this terrible pressure."

As the weeks wore on, however, it became clear that Lise was never going to reclaim her money from Berlin. This time the government said that she was not entitled to it because she had left the country illegally. Her clothes finally arrived in Sweden in October, but she had to pay a substantial customs tax to receive them, something she could ill afford to do. "My salary is such that I can pay for my room, food, and small daily expenses like bus fare, postage, etc., only by being very thrifty," she complained to Otto in a letter. "Stockholm is very expensive, and I dare not think of what might happen if I should become sick."

The reality of her new situation began to slowly sink in. Although she was familiar with Siegbahn's ground-breaking work in x-ray spectroscopy, Lise had never realized, until she came to Sweden, how he had struggled for years in Sweden to get funding for his own equipment and other scientists to help him. Moreover, he was eight years younger than she, and he regarded her ideas about physics as somewhat outdated. He did not consider her a true colleague or include her in his work, nor did he give her the equipment and assistants for her to set up her own laboratory.

Despite all of this, Lise knew she was lucky to be out of Germany. The conditions for Jews worsened every day. The Reich had liquidated their businesses and taken away the licenses of Jewish doctors and lawyers to practice. They required all Jews to register their property, pay special taxes, carry special identity cards, and even assume the middle names of "Sara" or "Israel" so that they could be easily recognized and ridiculed.

Then, on November 9 and 10, mobs of ordinary Germans went wild in the streets. They attacked Jews, destroyed their homes and businesses, and even burned their synagogues to the ground. Shattered glass filled the streets, and this event became known as "Kristallnacht," German for crystal night.

Even more frightening, the government had rounded up 30,000 Jewish men and put them in concentration camps. The only way they could be released was if they emigrated to another country. Of course, the

Germans knew this was virtually impossible. Other countries, afraid they would be deluged by more Jews than they could accommodate with food, lodging, and jobs, were beginning to close their borders to immigrants.

Meanwhile, Otto and Fritz Strassman had continued the uranium experiments, although they remained puzzled by the results. On a trip through Denmark, Otto stopped in Copenhagen, where Lise met him for breakfast so that they could discuss the problems.

By now, Otto and Fritz had reached the conclusion that the new substance in the radioactive mixture must be an *isotope* of radium. An isotope is an atom of any element, such as radium, that has the same number of protons but a different number of neutrons.

Lise was not convinced. She urged Otto to keep probing. Back in Berlin, he and Fritz continued with the experiments, and eventually Lise's scepticism proved correct. They were forced to conclude that the "new" substance was actually barium instead of a new element. But this introduced another problem: How did the barium get into the mixture? "We know uranium cannot really break up into barium!" Otto wrote to Lise.

But Lise was not so sure. Could an atom of one element split into two lighter, separate elements? It was unthinkable, but Lise could come up with no other explanation. "One cannot unconditionally say: it is impossible," she wrote back.

Otto and Fritz began a new round of experiments. Fritz later said that this was because of Lise's letter. "Fortunately L. Meitner's opinion and judgment carried so much weight with us in Berlin that the necessary control experiments were immediately undertaken," he wrote. He added that they always regarded Lise as the intellectual leader of their team, even though she was now in Sweden and could no longer be with them in their laboratory.

Otto was having his own share of problems. A rumor circulated that he had Jewish ancestors. He was able to prove that this was not true, but it caused him a great deal of anxiety. Meanwhile, he continued to fill out more papers, trying to get the German goverment to release Lise's pension money. His efforts were unsuccessful. The Germans wanted to wipe out the Jews forever—but not before seizing their money.

At Christmastime, Lise went to western Sweden to visit a friend. Her nephew, Otto Robert Frisch, met her there. He came out of his hotel room one night to find his Aunt Lise engrossed in a letter. "I wanted to discuss with her a new experiment that I was planning, but she wouldn't listen," he later wrote.

Lise showed him a letter from Otto, which asked Lise for her help in figuring out if indeed a uranium atom could split. There, in the dark, Lise and her nephew began figuring out how to prove this by using

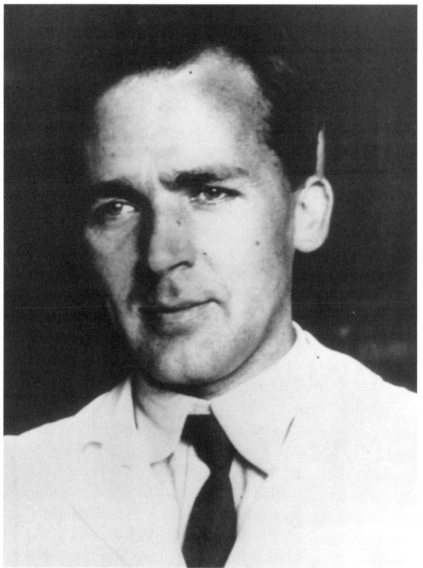

Fritz Strassman acknowledged Lise's instrumental leadership in the discovery of nuclear fission after she had fled Germany.

the laws and mathematical formulas of physics. They paced back and forth in the snow, he on skis and she on foot.

They decided that if it was true that a uranium atom could split, it would not be an abrupt chipping or cracking. Earlier, scientist Niels Bohr had speculated that an atom was like a drop of water. If he was correct, an atom's split would be somewhat wobbly—like one drop of water shakily splitting into two drops.

Lise and Otto Robert knew that in the split second before a drop of water splits, it must overcome the surface tension of the drop that attempts to hold it together. But the nuclei of atoms differ from a water droplet in an important way: they are electrically charged. Lise and Otto Robert theorized that these charges might cancel out the effect of the surface tension holding the nucleus together. Of course, Otto Robert later wrote, "When the two drops separated they would be driven apart by their mutual electric repulsion and would acquire a very large energy."

Einstein, in his famous theory of relativity, had stated that energy is created when mass disappears. Lise and Otto Robert sat on the tree trunk, furiously scribbling long, complex mathematical formulas from memory. Their calculations, along with Einstein's theory, showed that it was possible that a nucleus could split. The mass of the two new atoms added together would be less than that of the original atom, however, because some mass would be burned up in the process. The energy given off would repel the two atoms apart from each other and overcome the surface tension holding the original atom together. Using physics, Lise and Otto Robert had proven that an atom could split.

Otto Hahn and Fritz Strassmann published their article proclaiming that they had split the atom, and a few weeks later, Lise and Otto Robert published one of their own that explained how the split occurred. They also gave the new phenomenon a name: nuclear fission.

The discovery sent shock waves through the scientific community worldwide. If atoms could be split under controlled conditions, there would be endless possibilities for what could be done with this new energy.

Otto and Fritz did not put Lise's name on the article they published. They could not admit, without endangering their lives in Germany, that they had continued to work with Lise.

Still, after all of her years of work with Otto, the fact that she could not claim any credit for the discovery was a bitter pill for Lise to swallow. Siegbahn did not even congratulate her and continued to treat her coldly. Although Lise had many ideas for follow-up experiments, he refused to give her the equipment she needed to conduct them.

To Otto, she wrote: "With me things are not good at

all. I have a place to work here but no position that gives me the least right to do anything....Forgive this unhappy letter. I never wrote how bad it really is. Sometimes I do not know what to do with my life."

To her friend Eva von Bahr-Bergius, she wrote: "All these things weigh on me so, that I am losing all my self-confidence. I am making a real effort to hold on to my courage and I tell myself again and again that until now I have done very respectable physics. But under the current conditions I won't be able to do anything sensible and the fear of such an empty life never leaves me."

Meanwhile, Otto Hahn basked in his newfound fame. At last, he felt more confident that, thanks to his achievements, the Nazis would leave him and the institute alone. As the months wore on, Lise began to see a disturbing pattern in Otto's behavior. It seemed that he had gone beyond merely keeping her involvement in fission a secret for political reasons. He apparently had convinced himself and his colleagues in Germany that he deserved all the credit for the discovery.

Because his article had appeared before Lise's and her nephew's, it was easy for him to claim that the discovery was his alone, saying that Lise and Otto Robert had merely interpreted it. Otto, a chemist, said that it was chemistry that had led to the discovery—and that physics had had nothing to do with it. He told the same version of the story to Lise in a letter: "We absolutely never touched on physics, but instead we did chemical separations over and over again."

Lise was devastated. She had spent more than thirty years working with a man she considered one of her closest friends—and now he refused to acknowledge her contribution. Eventually, he began concealing the fact that he had ever worked with her.

Fritz Strassman would express a different view. "What difference does it make that Lise Meitner did not directly participate in the 'discovery?'" he later wrote. "Her initiative was the beginning of the joint work with Hahn—4 years later she belonged to our team—and she was bound to us intellectually from Sweden. [She] was the intellectual leader of our team, and therefore she belonged to us—even if she was not present for the 'discovery of fission.'"

The Germans were quick to realize just how nuclear fission could benefit them. If they could harness the energy of millions of splitting atoms, they could build a devastating bomb. Although Otto did not volunteer his services to the Nazis, he did not turn them away when they asked for his help.

And by now, the Germans had a need for his help. On September 1, 1939, Hitler's army attacked Poland at dawn. Two days later, France and England declared war on Germany.

Chapter Eight

In Otto's Shadow

Despite the growing strain between Otto and Lise, he remained her closest friend in Berlin—and the only person who might be able to rescue her belongings and send them to Sweden. After nine months in a small hotel room without her furniture, most of her clothes, and her books and scientific papers, Lise was growing anxious.

Otto wrote to assure her that he was doing all he could. "You must think we haven't done a thing, but the opposite is true," he said. "After the official expert examined your things, your silver, etc., we thought it would go quickly. Then came a new order that all books, etc. must be examined. That couldn't be done without a list of every book and publisher....After many telephone calls to the Literature Office, they turned us over to the superior authority: the Ministry of Propaganda....Tomorrow two men will finally come to inspect all your books."

Before they arrived, Otto searched through the

books himself, removing any he thought the inspectors would not approve of. Even so, they took away quite a few more, calling them "forbidden/undesirable or of importance to the state."

In May, almost a year after her escape, a bewildered Swedish mover drove his truck to Lise's apartment and began unloading furniture that had been chopped into splinters. Her bed was broken, and books with torn pages were thrown among the furniture. Instead of taking the glasses and dishes out of her china cabinet, the German movers had simply shoved the full cabinet in the truck, allowing everything inside to tumble over and shatter.

Lise was heartbroken, but she knew that she was better off in Sweden. By now, one-third of all Jews had fled Germany. The ones who remained were facing tiny food rations, forced labor, and special taxes. They were required to live in special housing, which isolated them from everyone else. They could not even use public transportation or telephones.

As usual, Lise turned to her work for comfort. She was still interested in doing further research on the transuranics, and the race was on to discover a new element, which would be ninety-three on the periodic table of elements. But her relationship with Manne Siegbahn, the director of the institute in Sweden, remained cold and tense, and this affected her work.

Some of the friction between them was due to jealousy. Lise's reputation in the scientific community and her accomplishments overshadowed Siegbahn's own. She was also an outspoken woman, something that was not fully accepted in the late 1930s. It didn't help that Lise's friends were usually people that Siegbahn also didn't like. She was safe from the terrible tragedies in Germany, but she would never be truly a part of his institute.

Frustrated with the situation in Sweden, she decided to travel to Copenhagen, Denmark, to do further experiments. At the laboratory there, a new piece of equipment, the *cyclotron*, would make the process of creating nuclear chain reactions much faster and easier.

The morning after Lise arrived in Copenhagen, German planes swooped into the country. Denmark had signed a non-aggression pact with Hitler, thinking that would stop him from invading the country. Now Hitler was violating the agreement, and Denmark had not prepared itself for a war. The country surrendered without a fight. Fortunately, the Germans did not seem anxious to force Jews out of Denmark, so Lise was able to remain for three weeks to do her experiments. But scientists in Berkeley, California, beat her to the discovery of the ninety-third element, neptunium.

It was yet another disappointment, but Lise turned her attention to helping other Jews escape from Germany and Austria. All Jews ages six and older were now required to wear large, yellow Stars of David on their clothing whenever they appeared in public so that everyone would know they were Jews. Massive numbers of Jews were being shipped by train to mysterious work camps in Poland and an enormous number of them were dying there. Years later, it would become apparent that this was the beginning of the Holocaust.

In Berlin, the Germans were not only trying to wipe out the Jews, but even the memory of them—by destroying any records of their accomplishments or their very existence. Otto continued to get all of the credit for the discoveries he and Lise had made together—even the work they had done long before the rise of the Nazis.

By late 1941, much of the world was once again at war. The old Allies from World War I, England and France, were once again leading a host of nations fighting Germany. This time Italy and Japan were fighting on Germany's side. On December 7, 1941, the Japanese made a mistake that would change history: they attacked Pearl Harbor, Hawaii. Now the United States was drawn into the war against the Axis Powers; Germany, Italy, and Japan.

It seemed that none of Lise's friends were safe any longer. The Allies were bombing her relatives in Berlin. Her relatives in England were being bombed by the Germans. The Costers, who had been so kind in helping her escape, were nearly starving to death in Holland. Lise sent them food. The government of

Sweden, although it was not fighting in the war, now officially opened its borders to Jewish refugees and even gave them housing and an allowance.

Although Lise continued to do all she could to help her friends, her relationships were tense and strained. Although she still loved Germany, Lise felt it was important that all "good Germans" wish for Hitler's— and Germany's—defeat in the war. She did not refrain from expressing this in her letters.

Many of her friends, especially Otto, were not willing to make a public stand. He wrote to Lise less often, and when he did, he stuck to very narrow, personal topics, such as his and Edith's health. Lise's friendship with Elisabeth Schiemann had also become strained. All of it saddened Lise. "It takes half or even a whole lifetime to make a few friends, and then one loses them in the blink of an eye," she lamented.

Jewish scientists who had fled Germany and were now living in England and the United States felt increasingly worried that the Germans would use fission to develop bombs. Albert Einstein wrote a letter to American President Franklin D. Roosevelt warning him of the danger. Roosevelt ordered American scientists to begin work on such a bomb, too. This became known as the Manhattan Project.

In Birmingham, England, Lise's nephew, Otto Robert, was working on a similar project. He was invited to go to the United States to work on the project there. He made certain that his Aunt Lise received an invitation, too.

To most scientists in Lise's situation—forced from her home and friends, working in an institute where she was an unwelcome outsider—the offer would have been tempting. Here was a chance to once again participate in ground-breaking physics. For Lise, however, the answer was simple. She was repulsed by the very idea of working on a bomb project.

By 1943, Lise felt more isolated than ever. She had chosen not to join the Allies' bomb project, but she could not side with the Germans, either. This strained her friendships even further. When Otto Hahn came to Sweden for a visit, Lise tried to persuade him that all "good Germans," particularly well-known scientists, were partially responsible for what was happening because they had not publicly spoken out against the Nazis. Otto felt that Lise was being unreasonable. It was a point of contention they would never resolve.

To Eva von Bahr-Bergius, Lise wrote: "The letters from German friends sound very depressed, yet I do not think they comprehend just what sort of fate has befallen Germany through their passivity. And they understand even less that they share responsibility for the horrible crimes Germany has committed. These thoughts make me terribly unhappy. How shall the world trust a new Germany when its best and intellectually most promising people do not have the insight to understand this and do not have a burning desire to make whatever amends are possible?"

In 1944, Otto was secretly awarded the Nobel Prize, the world's highest scientific honor, for the discovery of nuclear fission. Lise was not recognized. Otto's selection was kept secret for a time, because Germans were forbidden to accept awards in the midst of World War II.

Germany's involvement in the war ended just a few months later, in early 1945. Hitler, in an attempt to overrun most of Europe, had grossly miscalculated what his troops could accomplish. He had ordered them to invade Russia, not realizing that his men were ill prepared to fight in bone-chilling winter weather in such a huge territory. Many of the German troops froze or starved to death, yet Hitler refused to let them turn back. Meanwhile, the Allies were pushing back German armies that had invaded Africa and other parts of Europe. With the Allies closing in around him, Hitler, unable to accept such a crushing defeat, committed suicide on April 30, 1945.

As the Allies recaptured land the Germans had taken, they discovered something horrifying in the mysterious concentration camps. In an attempt to annihilate everyone the Germans considered "inferior," six million Jews—and five million people from other races, such as Poles and Gypsies—had been gassed, starved, or shot to death. Their bones were buried in huge piles in mass graves. The Germans had picked through their belongings, taking their jewelry and even the gold fillings from their teeth. The people who remained alive were little more than skeletons with skin stretched tightly across their bones, starving to death and sick with diseases that had swept through the camps.

Considering all of this, and her own personal struggles in Sweden, not winning the Nobel seemed relatively unimportant to Lise. However, she was about to receive more fame and recognition than she had ever expected—but for all the wrong reasons.

On August 7, 1945, while Lise was vacationing in the Swedish countryside, the telephone rang. It was a reporter from a Swedish newspaper. He told her the ominous news: "The first uranium bomb has been used over Hiroshima [Japan], said to be the equivalent of 20,000 tons of ordinary explosives." American President Harry S. Truman had given the order for the Americans to drop the bomb on the Japanese, who had continued with the war even after Germany and Italy surrendered.

Lise ran out of the house and spent the next five hours walking through the woods and fields alone, unable to believe what had become of her proud discovery. When she returned to her hotel, she found a huge stack of telephone messages—all from reporters. They flooded into a nearby boardinghouse and camped out on the doorstep of her hotel, waiting for her to emerge.

Lise said little to the reporters, except that she knew nothing about the bomb. That did not satisfy them, and some invented interviews with her and published them in their newspapers. They followed her around, taking her photograph whenever they could. One newspaper ran her photo with a caption that said: "FLEEING JEWESS." The article portrayed her as a Jewish refugee who had given the blueprint for the bomb to the Allies.

In the days that followed, it was easy to see why there was so much interest. The bomb had destroyed five square miles of Hiroshima, killing between 70,000 and 100,000 people. A second bomb had been dropped on Nagasaki, Japan, as well, with similar consequences.

Lise was distraught. She had wanted nothing to do with the bomb. She and Otto had discovered nuclear fission almost by accident, never thinking that it would lead to such a weapon of mass destruction. Now the Jewish community openly embraced her, proud to call her one of their own. But this upset Lise even more. She had never thought of herself as a Jew.

Lise was not alone in her discomfort. The scientists who had worked for the Allies, including Otto Robert, now had a difficult time reading about the devastating misery that their invention had caused.

Now that the war was over, Allied troops were occupying much of Europe. Intelligence officers forced Otto Hahn and other prominent German scientists to go to England. Although they were there against their will, they were given luxurious accommodations at Farm Hall, a country estate in England. Their captors said they were seizing the scientists to make sure they were not building any more bombs, but they actually had another motive. They had bugged the entire estate with hidden microphones so that they could record the scientists' conversations.

All of these taped conversations later became public. Otto and others were heard discussing how terrible Hitler was, but expressing openly how they wished Germany had won the war. In smug, self-righteous banter, they concluded that they didn't discover the bomb first because they simply didn't want to invent such a terrible weapon. They scarcely mentioned how hard they had tried.

The truth was that the Allies had beaten the German scientists in the bomb race, fair and square. One British officer who listened to the tapes noted that Otto and the others seemed to consider the war a "misfortune forced on the Germans by the malignancy of the Western Powers, who should by now have forgotten that it had taken place (the guests seem to have done so) and that the United Nations should be largely concerned to set Germany on her feet again."

The irony was that Otto was quite jealous of the attention Lise was receiving because of the bomb, even though she herself did not want it. Otto stuck to his story that the discovery of fission was due to chemistry, not physics, and that Lise had little to do with it. In fact, he brazenly said that she had steered him and Fritz Strassman away from the discovery, and that it was only after she left Berlin and was no longer hampering their investigation that they discovered fission.

All Lise could discern was that Otto had either decided to lie, or he had truly convinced himself that this was the case. No one would ever know his true motives, because he continued to say this until he died. Although the war was over, and there was no reason to continue to distance himself from Lise, he never changed his story.

Chapter Nine

Reconciliation

Now that the war was over, a formal Nobel Prize ceremony was held for Otto Hahn. There was enough controversy over whether Otto alone deserved the prize to prompt the Nobel committee to review its earlier decision. In the end, the committee voted to give it to him. This more than anything else cemented his version of the fission discovery. Whenever it was written about, Lise was mentioned only as one of Otto's assistants. The Nobel committee did not name Fritz Strassman as a recipient, either.

Lise wrote bitterly to a friend: "Surely Hahn fully deserved the Nobel Prize in chemistry. There is really no doubt about it. But I believe that [Otto Robert] Frisch and I contributed something not insignificant to the clarification of the process of uranium fission—how it originates and that it produces so much energy, and that was something very remote from Hahn. For this reason I find it a bit unjust that in newspapers I was called a Mitarbeiterin [assistant] of Hahn's in the same sense that Strassman was."

Lise's supporters were outraged. But there was still a chance that she could receive a Nobel Prize in physics. Niels Bohr nominated Lise and Otto Robert for the physics prize in 1946, then for the chemistry prize in 1947 and 1948. They never received enough votes from the committee.

Many of Lise's supporters came to believe that this was partly because Siegbahn, her Swedish supervisor, was one of the committee members. In fact, they began to bitterly regret that she had ever gone to Sweden. It seemed that, had she gone to work for anyone other than Siegbahn, she might have received the prize.

Lise did receive some of the recognition she deserved elsewhere. In early1946, she was invited to be a visiting professor at the Catholic University of America in Washington, D.C.

It was her first trip to the United States. As she stepped off the plane, a swarm of reporters and photographers surrounded the woman they had come to regard a pioneer of the atomic bomb.

While in the United States, Lise was named "Woman of the Year" by the Women's National Press Club. At the banquet, she sat next to President Truman, who presented her with an inscribed silver bowl. Lise accepted with a smile and a bow, but was grateful that she was not forced to give a speech. In addition to her natural shyness, she also worried that her English would not be good enough. Truman gave a speech call-

Lise Meitner met President Harry Truman when she was named "Woman of the Year" by the Women's National Press Club.

ing for food to be sent to war-ravaged Europe.

On the day of Lise's first lecture in America, four hundred people crowded into a room at Catholic University to hear her. The invitations to speak elsewhere came pouring in. She talked to high school students, gave seminars at other universities, talked to women's groups, and received honorary doctorates from several universities. Although she was a small, thin woman with a humble manner and a gentle voice, her command of physics was unmistakable to those who heard her speak.

Everywhere she went, strangers stopped her on the street. Waitresses and taxi drivers asked for her autograph. Metro-Goldwyn-Mayer Studios in Hollywood even wanted to make a movie of her life, but Lise was outraged when she read the script. "It is based on the stupid newspaper story that I left Germany with the bomb in my purse.... I answered that it was against my innermost convictions to be shown in a film, and pointed out the errors in their story." MGM executives apparently thought Lise was simply holding out for more money, but when they made a bigger offer, Lise lost her temper and threatened to sue them! Throughout the rest of her life, she refused to give anyone permission to write her biography or any plays or movie scripts based on her life.

Meanwhile, Otto had been released from Farm Hall and returned to Germany, where he was named president of the German professional society for scientists. His letters to Lise described the miseries of post-war Germany—shortages of food, coffee, cocoa, and cigars, travel restrictions, little money for heating fuel, and conflicts with British and American officials who were occupying Germany as part of the peace agreement.

Lise wrote back expressing her sympathy, but reminding him that the Germans had inflicted misery on millions of people and in fact deserved their predicament. "If the best Germans do not understand now what has happened and what must never happen again, who should instruct young people that the path that was tried was tragic for Germany and the world?"

For the rest of her life, Lise would be frustrated with Otto and other German friends who never admitted that Germany had been wrong. Otto, now famous as a Nobel laureate, received many invitations to speak abroad, and he never failed to use those occasions as an opportunity to complain about how badly Germany was suffering.

Despite her irritation, Lise maintained a strained friendship with Otto. After all these years, and despite his betrayal of her, she could never bear to cut him off altogether. They simply had been through too much together.

Lise was able to leave Siegbahn's institute in 1947 for a new position in her own laboratory at the Royal Institute of Technology in Sweden. The director, Gudmund Borelius, very much wanted Lise to work there and wholeheartedly supported further research in nuclear physics.

Although she was grateful for a better work environment, Lise would never feel truly at home in Sweden. She continued to write and send clothing, shoes, and household items to her friends in Germany. For Otto's birthday, she mailed him sugar, cigars, and cigarettes—luxury items that were scarce there.

As part of the settlement of the war, the Allies required that all Germans declare their previous affiliation with the Nazis. Ironically, the same Nazi activists who had surrounded Lise during her last years at the

Institute in Berlin were now in danger of losing their jobs, being demoted, and even going to prison. Germans were allowed to submit affidavits from well-known people in their defense, and some of her former colleagues now wrote to Lise Meitner, asking her to vouch for them.

Reluctantly, Lise wrote letters on behalf of a few of them. In some ways, she viewed the Allies' process of "Denazification" as horribly similar to what the Nazis had done to the Jews. She refused to testify against any of them.

Lise could not bring herself to return to Germany for several years, and then it was only to attend Max Planck's funeral. As she passed through Germany on a train, she saw through the windows heaps of rubble where there had once been towns.

Unexpectedly, Fritz Strassman, Otto's former partner, asked her to consider returning to the old institute in Berlin to become head of the physics department and director of the institute—the very position that Otto had held. Lise considered it for a short time but then refused. Although she was flattered by the offer, she had no desire to ever live in Germany again.

To her friend Eva, she wrote: "I personally believe that I cannot live in Germany. From all I see in letters from my German friends, and other things I hear about Germany, the Germans still do not comprehend what has happened, and they have completely forgotten all the horrors that did not personally happen to them. I think I would not be able to breathe in such an atmosphere."

Another milestone in Lise's life was receiving the Max Planck Medal from the German Chemical Society. This was particularly special to Lise because of her love and admiration of Planck. Also, she saw it as a tie to "the old Germany that I loved very much, the Germany to which I can hardly be grateful enough for the crucial years of my scientific development, for the deep pleasure in scientific work and a very dear circle of friends."

Lise continued her research until she was well into her seventies. Along with Sigvard Eklund, she helped build Sweden's first nuclear reactor and recruited many promising young physicists and engineers to build Sweden's program in nuclear research. Sweden had never been, and would never be, a producer of nuclear weapons. Instead, the country concentrated on using the technology to build nuclear reactors that generate electricity, something to which Lise was proud to contribute.

In 1954, at the age of seventy-five, Lise retired and took an office at Eklund's laboratory, housed over the new underground reactor, which was nearly complete. She spent her time writing and following new developments in physics. The next year, she became the first recipient of the Otto Hahn Prize, named for her friend and rival.

In 1960, at the age of eighty-two, Lise moved to Cambridge, England, to be close to Otto Robert and his family. A long and distinguished career had come to a close.

Throughout the last years of her life, many people asked Lise to write her autobiography, or to at least contribute to a biography of herself written by someone else. A private person, she remained uninterested. Biographies of people who were still alive, she said, were "either insincere or tactless, usually both." Fortunately, she preserved her scientific papers and diaries and kept much of her correspondence.

Until his death, Otto continued to suppress the past and deny Lise's contribution to his work. He was awarded countless honors, medals, and keys to cities. His face was on a stamp, and buildings and schools were named after him. Even after his death, bridges and plazas were built that bore his name.

In 1958, a new German institute for nuclear research was built in the town of Wannsee on the outskirts of Berlin. At first, everyone wanted to name it only for Otto Hahn. But Lise's supporters prevailed, and it was named the "Hahn-Meitner-Institut fur Kernforschung" (Hahn-Meitner Institute for Nuclear Research). At a dedication ceremony in March 1959, the mayor praised Lise and noted that she "had not been spared bitter suffering." That, he said, was reason to thank her "all the more" for the work she had done in Berlin.

Although Lise Meitner addressed her discontent with Otto Hahn in her letters to him, she never publicly spoke against him.

This honor helped Lise feel better about her past in Germany, but it did not undo the years of being in Otto's shadow. In accounts of how fission was discovered, she continued to be referred to only as his assistant.

Lise had tried a number of times to get Otto to correct this misperception to no avail. In 1953, she said to him in a letter: "In 1917 I was officially entrusted by the directors of the KWI for Chemistry to create the physics section, and I headed it for 21 years. Try for once to imagine yourself in my place! What would you say if you were only characterized as the 'longtime Mitarbeiter' of me? After the last 15 years, which I wouldn't wish on any good friend, shall my scientific past also be taken from me? Is that fair? And why is it happening?"

Otto never answered those questions, nor did he correct the record in a book he wrote about his life. Lise did not press the matter further. In fact, some of her friends later said they believed that she did not want to be known simply for the fission discovery— particularly since it had led to the development of nuclear weapons.

Otto's version of the fission discovery became a permanent part of the Deutsches Museum, a science and technology museum in Munich, Germany. Encased in the museum are samples of the equipment, much of it built by Lise herself, used in the experiments that led to the discovery of nuclear fission. A sign talks mostly of Otto and mentions Fritz Strassman in passing. It was not until thirty years later, when the public criticized the exhibit, that a small sign with Lise's name was added. But it, too, refers to her as Otto's Mitarbeiterin.

Lise did not allow bitterness over these things to dominate her life. She remained a person who enjoyed friendships and helping others, even as old age and sickness began to overtake her.

In 1963, she reflected on her fifty years in physics to a group of college students in Vienna, Austria. She talked joyfully of her career, describing physics and the "great and lovable personalities" she had come to know as a "magic musical accompaniment to life." When she finished, the enthusiastic crowd swarmed around the frail, tiny, eighty-five-year-old woman.

In Cambridge, England, Otto Robert, his wife Ulla, and their two children made Lise feel a part of their home. Otto Robert played piano for his aunt and talked to her about physics. The field continued to advance so rapidly, however, that by the time she was in her mid-eighties, it was difficult for Lise Meitner to understand the new formulas. In 1964, she suffered a heart attack, and her health became too frail for her to travel.

Two years later, Lise, Otto Hahn, and Fritz Strassman were awarded the U.S. Atomic Energy Commission's Enrico Fermi Prize for their contributions to the discovery of fission. Neither Otto nor Lise were well enough to travel to Washington, so the award ceremony was held in Vienna. Even so, Lise was too ill to attend, so Otto Robert accepted the award for her. After all the years that had transpired, Otto Hahn continued to say that the discovery belonged only to chemistry. He actually suggested that Fritz Strassman alone receive the prize! Fortunately for Lise, the awards committee did not follow his advice.

In 1967, Lise fell and broke her hip. She also suffered a series of small strokes that made it nearly impossible for her to speak. She spent the last few months of her life in a nursing home, mostly unaware of her surroundings. Otto Robert did not have the heart to tell her when he received word that Otto Hahn had passed away on July 28, 1968. Almost three months later, Lise died peacefully in her sleep on October 27, 1968, just shy of her ninetieth birthday.

Just as she would have wanted, her burial service was simple. Only her family attended, and there were no long-winded eulogies about her life.

Otto Robert's simple inscription on his aunt's gravestone told her story in a few powerful words: "Lise Meitner: a physicist who never lost her humanity."

Glossary

atomic number: the number of protons and electrons in an atom.

cyclotron: an instrument for accelerating atomic particles with electricity.

electron: a negatively-charged subatomic particle that orbits the nucleus of an atom.

isotope: an atom of a particular element that contains a different number of neutrons, and therefore has a different atomic mass, but still retains the same chemical properties of the original element.

mass number: the number of neutrons and protons in an atom.

neutron: a non-charged subatomic particle found in the nucleus of an atom.
nuclear fission: the splitting of a nucleus into two parts, resulting in a release of energy.

periodic table of elements: a chart of all known chemical elements arranged in rows by atomic number.
proton: a positively-charged subatomic particle within the nucleus of an atom.

radiation: energy in the form of moving subatomic particles or waves.

transuranics: Enrico Fermi's name for the elements he thought were produced when uranium is bombarded with neutrons. In fact, they are not new elements, but barium isotopes.
theory of relativity: states that all observed motion and energy is regulated by the properties of space and time.

x-ray spectroscopy: the study of x-ray wavelengths.

Timeline

1878—born November 7 in Vienna, Austria.

1902—enters the University of Vienna.

1906—receives doctorate in physics, graduating *summa cum laude.*

1907—begins experiments with Otto Hahn in Berlin.

1913—Laboratorium Hahn-Meitner is founded.

1915—serves in German medical corps during WWI.

1917—Laboratorium Meitner is founded.

1918—discovers proactinium.

1919—named first woman professor in Germany.

1934—publishes first article on "transuranics" with Fritz Strassman and Otto Hahn.

1938—passport is revoked.

　　　—escapes to Sweden.

　　　—publishes article on nuclear fission with nephew.

1944—Otto Hahn is secretly awarded Nobel Prize for the discovery of nuclear fission.

1946—visits United States; named "Woman of the Year."

1947—receives Max Planck Medal.

1954—retires.

1955—receives Otto Hahn Prize.

1958—Hahn-Meitner Institut fur Kernforschung is completed in Wannsee, Germany.

1960—moves to Cambridge, England, to be with family.

1964—suffers heart attack.

1966—awarded Enrico Fermi Prize.

1968—dies in Cambridge, England.

Bibliography

Badash, Lawrence, ed. Rutherford and Boltwood: *Letters on Radioactivity*. New Haven: Yale UP, 1969.

Broda, Englebert. *Ludwig Boltzmann*. Trans. Lary Gay and Engelbert Broda. Woodbridge, CT.: Oxbow Press, 1983.

Dictionary of Physics. Chicago: NTC Publishing Group, 1996.

Frisch, O.R. "The Interest Is Focusing on the Atomic Nucleus." S. Rozental, ed., *Niels Bohr: His Life and World as Seen by His Friends and Colleagues*. Amsterdam: North Holland/New York: John Wiley, 1967.

Hahn, Otto. *A Scientific Autobiography*. Trans. Willy Ley. New York: Charles Scribner's Sons, 1996.

Meitner, Lise. "Looking Back," *Bulletin of the Atomic Scientist*, Vol. 20, Nov. 1964.

Operation Epsilon: The Farm Hall Transcripts. Berkeley: U. of California Press, 1993.

Sime, Ruth Lewin. *Lise Meitner: A Life in Physics*. Berkeley: U. of California Press, 1996.

—."Lise Meitner and the Discovery of Nuclear Fission," *Scientific American*, Jan. 1998.

—."Lise Meitner's escape from Germany,"*American Journal of Physics*, Mar. 1990.

Sources

CHAPTER ONE

p. 10, "We were shaking with fear..." Sime, Ruth Lewin. *Lise Meitner: A Life in Physics*. Berkeley and Los Angeles: U. of California Press, 1996, p. 204.

p. 11, "heartiest congratulations..." Ibid., p. 205.

CHAPTER TWO

p. 14, "the unusual goodness..." Ibid., p. 4.

p. 14, "an eight-year-old..." Ibid., p. 5.

p. 18, "Many parents shared..." Sime, op.cit., p. 9.

p. 18, "I was really afraid..." Meitner, Lise. "Looking Back," *Bulletin of the Atomic Scientist*, Nov. 1964, p. 3.

p. 20, "all I have..." Broda, Englebert. Ludwig Boltzmann. Trans. Lary Gay and Engelbert Broda. Woodbridge, CT.: Oxbow Press, 1983, p. 14.

p. 22, "Ach, how dumb of me!" Ibid., p. 12.

p. 22, "pure soul'..." Sime, op.cit., p. 14.

CHAPTER THREE

p. 28, "it can not be..." Sime, Ibid., p. 26.

p. 32, "Oh, I thought you were a man," Meitner, op.cit., p. 5.

p. 32, "a young lady..." Badash, Lawrence, ed. Rutherford and Boltwood: *Letters on Radioactivity*. New Haven: Yale UP, 1969, p. 206.

p. 34, "had had a strict..." Sime, op.cit., pp. 34-35.

p. 34, "would not think..." Hahn, Otto. *A Scientific Autobiography*. Trans. Willy Ley. New York: Charles Scribner's Sons, 1996, p. 65.

p. 34, "7 blouses..." Sime, op.cit., p. 36.

p. 36, "I love physics..." Ibid., p. 45.

CHAPTER FOUR

p. 39, "My mother's apartment..." Ibid., p. 53.

p. 40, "First, you were not asked..." Ibid., p. 58.

p. 41, "I never expected..." Ibid., p. 60.

p. 41, "Today we amputated..." Ibid., p. 60.

p. 41, "I would like..." Ibid., p. 61.

p. 42, "I never had time for it!" Ibid., p. 35.

p. 42, "I feel superfluous." Ibid., p. 61.

p. 44, "We have succeeded...," Ibid., p. 70.

CHAPTER FIVE

p. 46, "Milk and meat..." Ibid., p. 76.

p. 49, "There really is enough to eat," Ibid., p. 98.

p. 50, "At the moment..." Ibid., p. 108.

p. 52, "the human race..." Ibid., p. 119.

p. 55, "The political situation..." Sime, op.cit., p. 136.

p. 56, "The conduct of German..." Sime, op.cit., p. 138.

CHAPTER SIX

p. 62, "no need for further discussion." Sime, Ruth Lewin, "Lise Meitner and the Discovery of Nuclear Fission," *Scientific American*, Jan. 1998, p. 83.

p. 63, "The Jewess endangers..." Sime, op.cit., p. 184.

p. 65, "Political considerations..." Sime, Ruth Lewin. "Lise Meitner's escape from Germany." *American Journal of Physics*, Mar. 1990, p. 263.

p. 66, "the demands on me are such..." Ibid., p. 265.

p. 69, "We were shaking with fear..." Sime, op.cit., p. 204.

p. 69, "The danger consisted..." Ibid., p. 204.

p. 70, "Her sense of being inwardly torn apart..." Ibid., p. 205.

CHAPTER SEVEN

p. 72, "3 glass plates..." Ibid., p. 215.

p. 72, "I am not at all..." Ibid., p. 215.

p. 73, "Hopefully now..." Ibid., p. 217.

p. 73, "The laboratory is half deserted..." Ibid., p. 217.

p. 73, "My salary is such..." Ibid., p.220.

p. 75, "We know uranium..." Sime, *Scientific American*, p. 84.

p. 75, "One cannot unconditionally..." Ibid., p. 84.

p. 76, "Fortunately L. Meitner's..." Sime, op.cit., p. 229.

p. 76, "I wanted to discuss..." Frisch, O.R. "The Interest Is Focusing on the Atomic Nucleus." S. Rozental, ed., *Niels Bohr: His Life and World as Seen by His Friends and Colleagues*. Amsterdam: North Holland/New York, 1967, p. 143-148.

p. 78, "When the two drops separated..." Ibid., pp. 143-148.

p. 79, "With me things..." Sime, op.cit., pp. 254-255.

p. 80, "All these things weigh on me so..." Ibid., p. 257.

p. 80, "We absolutely..." Sime, *Scientific American*, p. 85.

p. 81, "What difference does it make..." Sime, op,cit., p. 241.

CHAPTER EIGHT

p. 82, "You must think..." Ibid., p. 268.

p. 83, "forbidden/undesirable...." , Ibid., p. 268.

p. 86, "It takes half...", Ibid., p. 294.

p. 87, "The letters from German..." Ibid., p. 308.

p. 89, "The first uranium bomb..." Ibid., p. 313.

p. 91, "misfortune forced on the Germans..." *Operation Epsilon: The Farm Hall Transcripts*. Berkeley: U. of California Press, 1993, p. 230.

CHAPTER NINE

p. 93, "Surely Hahn..." Sime, op.cit.., p. 327.

p. 96, "It is based..." Ibid., p. 332.

p. 96, "If the best Germans..." Ibid., p. 338.

p. 98, "I personally believe..." Ibid., p. 353-4.

p. 99, "the old Germany..." Ibid., p. 358.

p. 100, "either insincere or tactless..." Ibid., p. 363.

p. 100, "had not been spared..." Ibid., p. 369.

p. 102, "In 1917 I was officially entrusted..." Ibid., p. 370.

p. 103, "great and lovable personalities," Lise Meitner, "Looking Back,"*Bulletin of the Atomic Scientist*, Nov. 1964, p. 2.

p. 104, "Lise Meitner: a physicist..." Ibid., p. 380.

Index